# 25 MONTHS UNTIL COLLEGE

## The Don't Panic, Step-by-Step, What-When-Why-How Guide for Students and Parents

### Judy McNeely

College Pathfinders
820 Bay Avenue, Suite 230B
Capitola, CA 95010

Requests for bulk orders from libraries, guidance counselors and others should be mailed to the above address, requested at www.collegepathfinders.com, or emailed to judybookdoc@collegepathfinders.com.

Library of Congress Control Number: 2008934712

ISBN: 978-0-557-00880-3

# How To Use This Book

This book is written for students and their families. We break down the complicated process of applying to college into 25 months, starting in December of sophomore year. Often, there is only one task per month.

**Complicated, wordy books only add to the stress** of navigating the time line for admissions. This book is different: it breaks down generalities into small tasks. The few subjects requiring longer explanation are in the back of the book.

**Leave this book open to the month you're in, perhaps on your coffee table or kitchen table, with an extra copy for your bedroom. To keep stress levels down, do small tasks each month and use the spaces to take notes.**

My goal is to prevent you from missing deadlines by giving you a WHAT to do, WHEN, WHY and HOW. Too often students and parents say "We're afraid we'll miss crucial deadlines like the neighbor kid did."

Admissions officers will look at the forest AND the trees, but what if all the trees have similar grades and scores? The decision to admit can hinge on your attention to detail. 25 Months to the rescue! You CAN do this.

**Good luck getting admitted to the college of your dreams!**

Judy McNeely

**ATTENTION INTERNATIONAL STUDENTS:** Please note that most of the specific tasks covered in this book are geared to high schools in the United States. To meet American application deadlines, international students should read ahead to understand when deadlines fall, and make appropriate arrangements to meet them, whether by mail or online.

# MONTH

# 1

## DECEMBER

| 1 | 2 | 3 | 4 | 5 | 6 | 7 |
|---|---|---|---|---|---|---|
| 8 | 9 | 10 | 11 | 12 | 13 | 14 |
| 15 | 16 | 17 | 18 | 19 | 20 | 21 |
| 22 | 23 | 24 | 25 | 26 | 27 | 28 |

**Year:** | SOPHOMORE | JUNIOR | SENIOR |

# MONTH

## 1

### DECEMBER

| 1 | 2 | 3 | 4 | 5 | 6 | 7 |
|---|---|---|---|---|---|---|
| 8 | 9 | 10 | 11 | 12 | 13 | 14 |
| 15 | 16 | 17 | 18 | 19 | 20 | 21 |
| 22 | 23 | 24 | 25 | 26 | 27 | 28 |

**Year:** | **SOPHOMORE** | JUNIOR | SENIOR |

**WHAT** Research and apply for volunteer activities
**WHEN** Early December of sophomore year through senior year.
**WHY** While there's nothing wrong with personal activities like sports or paying jobs, colleges look for applicants willing to "give back" to the community.
**HOW** Use your local newspaper, the Internet and social networking sites (**facebook.com**, **myspace.com**, etc.) to identify public service programs. You don't have to become a different person—simply build on your current passions. Find areas which continue your personal interests, e.g. the student who loves horses works placing handicapped youth on horseback; the student who loves judo, teaches it to others. You don't have to go to distant places, either. There is no need to build houses in Mexico. A student who sees a need and solves a problem locally is more impressive than one who pays for an organization to set up a trip to a foreign country. Time spent near home can be more valued because you demonstrate initiative.

**Some web sites to consult for volunteer options:**
volunteermatch.com
networkforgood.org/volunteer
idealist.org

## Start Early

It looks less phony to care about a cause over a period of 25 months than to suddenly find a passion for helping the homeless in October of senior year.

# MONTH

# 1

## DECEMBER

| 1 | 2 | 3 | 4 | 5 | 6 | 7 |
|---|---|---|---|---|---|---|
| 8 | 9 | 10 | 11 | 12 | 13 | 14 |
| 15 | 16 | 17 | 18 | 19 | 20 | 21 |
| 22 | 23 | 24 | 25 | 26 | 27 | 28 |

## Year: | SOPHOMORE | JUNIOR | SENIOR |

**WHAT** Review your PSAT scores
(you took it in October)

**WHEN** Before the December break

**WHY** While standardized tests are down-played by some colleges, until there is a uniform system of grades nationwide, test scores will continue to play a big part in your admission to most colleges. The major value of your PSAT score is using it as a diagnostic tool.

**HOW** Get your scores from your high school counselor. This is the only test score NOT sent directly to your home address. This score is never seen by colleges. The PSAT score is used for analyzing weaknesses and provides a measure of your strengths as well as areas for you to work on. By identifying math and verbal areas where you have missed points, you can target specific skills to master over the next year.

**Reading** To increase your score, spend an hour daily reading fun stuff: newspapers, magazines, graphic novels, etc. The way to improve reading skills is not by solving "reading problems" but by reading.

**Math** Don't panic. Often, sophomore math students simply haven't covered the material yet.

**Writing** Because there is no writing on this preliminary SAT, we cover essay practice in January of junior year, Month 14, p. 37.

## How to Raise Your Score

To raise your score on standardized tests, your strategy should be slow and steady improvement over 15 to 17 months. This method yields far better results than an expensive crash course that you might be tempted to take just before the serious testing that will occur between March and June of your junior year.

# NOTES:

Your PSAT Scores:

Verbal _____

Math _____

Methods to improve scores:

_____

_____

_____

_____

_____

_____

_____

_____

_____

_____

# MONTH

# 2

## JANUARY

| 1 | 2 | 3 | 4 | 5 | 6 | 7 |
|---|---|---|---|---|---|---|
| 8 | 9 | 10 | 11 | 12 | 13 | 14 |
| 15 | 16 | 17 | 18 | 19 | 20 | 21 |
| 22 | 23 | 24 | 25 | 26 | 27 | 28 |

**Year:** | SOPHOMORE | JUNIOR | SENIOR |

# MONTH
# 2

**JANUARY**

| 1 | 2 | 3 | 4 | 5 | 6 | 7 |
| 8 | 9 | 10 | 11 | 12 | 13 | 14 |
| 15 | 16 | 17 | 18 | 19 | 20 | 21 |
| 22 | 23 | 24 | 25 | 26 | 27 | 28 |

## Year: | SOPHOMORE | JUNIOR | SENIOR

**WHAT** Look at topics for SAT Subject Tests. These are one-hour, multiple choice tests on specific topics, including science, math, languages, literature and history.

**WHEN** Begin studying in early January to take them in June.

**WHY** Most competitive colleges require two good SAT Subject scores, some require three. You will get a better score if you take the subject tests at the end of the school year in which you study the material, rather than waiting until the fall of senior year and re-learning the coursework. You will experience much less stress senior year if you get these tests out of the way sophomore and junior year.

**HOW** See **collegeboard.com.** Go to the bookstore to buy test prep books on your subjects. Begin now to take practice tests. You *can* raise your score significantly with self disciplined, independent study. You do not need a commercial course.

## Follow Your Class Work in the SAT Prep Book

One excellent method is to connect what is taught in class to the content in the prep book. If, by early May, your class hasn't covered an area that you see in the prep book, ask your teacher if the missing material will be covered in class. Find a tutor to do the original learning with, and be *sure* to take multiple practice tests.

# MONTH

**JANUARY**

| 1 | 2 | 3 | 4 | 5 | 6 | 7 |
| 8 | 9 | 10 | 11 | 12 | 13 | 14 |
| 15 | 16 | 17 | 18 | 19 | 20 | 21 |
| 22 | 23 | 24 | 25 | 26 | 27 | 28 |

**Year:** | **SOPHOMORE** | **JUNIOR** | **SENIOR** |

**WHAT** Plan college visits for spring break.

**WHEN** In January for spring break visits.

**WHY** Rather than rely solely on print and internet information, visiting colleges can be invaluable. There's nothing like setting foot on campus to get the feel of what it will be like to learn there. Over the 25 Months Until College, there are only two opportunities for extensive visits (complete with attending classes and staying in the dorms): spring breaks of sophomore year and junior year.

**HOW** Plan the itinerary by region. Contact admissions offices by e-mail or phone. Request and reserve tours, information sessions, possible dorm stays and class visits. You should take the 6 to 9 days of spring break for distant colleges, since nearby schools are easily seen in a long weekend. See **page 82** for more on college visits.

## Don't over-extend

Do not visit more than two colleges per day, because they begin to blur in your mind. You'll want to spend enough time at each college to really remember what it has to offer.

# MONTH

# 2

**JANUARY**

| | | | | | | |
|---|---|---|---|---|---|---|
| 1 | 2 | 3 | 4 | 5 | 6 | 7 |
| 8 | 9 | 10 | 11 | 12 | 13 | 14 |
| 15 | 16 | 17 | 18 | 19 | 20 | 21 |
| 22 | 23 | 24 | 25 | 26 | 27 | 28 |

## Year:  SOPHOMORE | JUNIOR | SENIOR

**WHAT** Begin to research scholarships available to high school students.

**WHEN** January of sophomore year through May of senior year.

**WHY** Many scholarships, especially those that are non-local, are open to grades 9-12.

**HOW** Using **fastweb.com** and **finaid.com**, search for scholarships. You will find many choices and many categories. Make copies of all scholarship information in your school counseling office that a junior can qualify for. Plus, check local high school websites frequently.

## Consider Essay Based Scholarships

Scholarships that require an essay are generally under-utilized and competition is usually less, so write an essay that you can use for multiple applications.

# MONTH
# 3

## FEBRUARY

| 1 | 2 | 3 | 4 | 5 | 6 | 7 |
|---|---|---|---|---|---|---|
| 8 | 9 | 10 | 11 | 12 | 13 | 14 |
| 15 | 16 | 17 | 18 | 19 | 20 | 21 |
| 22 | 23 | 24 | 25 | 26 | 27 | 28 |

**Year:** | SOPHOMORE | JUNIOR | SENIOR |

# MONTH
# 3

**FEBRUARY**

| 1 | 2 | 3 | 4 | 5 | 6 | 7 |
|---|---|---|---|---|---|---|
| 8 | 9 | 10 | 11 | 12 | 13 | 14 |
| 15 | 16 | 17 | 18 | 19 | 20 | 21 |
| 22 | 23 | 24 | 25 | 26 | 27 | 28 |

## Year: | SOPHOMORE | JUNIOR | SENIOR |

**WHAT Plan for your junior year courses.** Meet with your school counselor to identify the most rigorous course load offered for junior year classes.

**WHEN** Because students register for next year's classes in March or April, it is essential that you begin this discussion before the school's general registration process begins.

**WHY** Admissions officers want to know that you are willing to challenge yourself with coursework. They don't want to have you flunk out because college work is harder than anything you've experienced. Colleges care more about success in challenging courses than they do about high test scores. No matter how high your test scores are, it won't make up for an easy course load.

**HOW** Confirm with your school counselor that you will meet all the school's graduation requirements. Assess the school's offerings, and sign up for the most rigorous course load possible. When school starts next year, if you feel overwhelmed with these courses, step down to the regular class. For more about early action/early decision **see page 80.**

## College Courses Now?

Consider offerings at community colleges only if you cannot find "tough" courses at your high school. Academically challenging courses are called AP (Advanced Placement), IB (International Baccalaureate), Honors or Intensive.

# MONTH

# 4

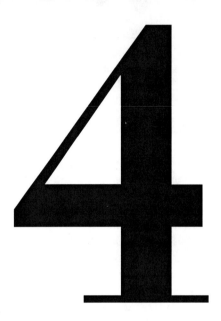

## MARCH

| 1 | 2 | 3 | 4 | 5 | 6 | 7 |
|---|---|---|---|---|---|---|
| 8 | 9 | 10 | 11 | 12 | 13 | 14 |
| 15 | 16 | 17 | 18 | 19 | 20 | 21 |
| 22 | 23 | 24 | 25 | 26 | 27 | 28 |

**Year:** | SOPHOMORE | JUNIOR | SENIOR |

# MONTH
# 4

**MARCH**

| 1 | 2 | 3 | 4 | 5 | 6 | 7 |
| 8 | 9 | 10 | 11 | 12 | 13 | 14 |
| 15 | 16 | 17 | 18 | 19 | 20 | 21 |
| 22 | 23 | 24 | 25 | 26 | 27 | 28 |

## Year: **SOPHOMORE** | JUNIOR | SENIOR

**WHAT**    Finalize junior year courses.
Explore summer offerings at local colleges.
Finalize plans for summer volunteering.

**WHEN**    Early March

**WHY**    Coursework is still the most important focus.

Show colleges that you can handle college level work plus delve more into your favorite subject.

Don't wait until summer because the good volunteering opportunities will be taken.

**HOW**    Check with your school counselor for all questions related to registration.

Visit the websites of colleges near you to find courses of interest.

Go to **volunteermatch.com, networkforgood.org/volunteer**, and **idealist.org** for volunteering ideas.

## Maximize Your Summer Volunteer Hours

Ask the administrator of your current volunteering project about the possibility of working more hours during the summer months.

# MONTH

**4**

## MARCH

| 1 | 2 | 3 | 4 | 5 | 6 | 7 |
| 8 | 9 | 10 | 11 | 12 | 13 | 14 |
| 15 | 16 | 17 | 18 | 19 | 20 | 21 |
| 22 | 23 | 24 | 25 | 26 | 27 | 28 |

**Year:** | SOPHOMORE | JUNIOR | SENIOR |

**WHAT** Narrow college choices to 25
**WHEN** Early March
**WHY** To allow you to plan an itinerary for college visits during spring break
**HOW** Use the books *The Fiske Guide to Colleges, Colleges That Change Lives, The Yale Insider's Guide* and *Cool Colleges.* Also visit the library, the counseling office at your school, and college websites.

## Narrowing Your Choices

It's time to clean out the clutter on your college list. Ask yourself why these schools are on your list and get rid of schools that are there only because a friend or relative likes them.

## {checklist}

### AND DON'T FORGET

- ☐ SAT Subject tests prep for June test date
- ☐ AP prep for May test dates [See page 78 for more on AP prep] Take practice tests now
- ☐ Continue volunteering.
- ☐ Continue to refine list of colleges for potential visits.

# NOTES:

Colleges to visit during spring break:

_____

_____

_____

_____

_____

Tours reserved:

_____

_____

_____

_____

Information session reserved:

_____

_____

_____

_____

# MONTH

# 5

## APRIL

| | | | | | | |
|---|---|---|---|---|---|---|
| 1 | 2 | 3 | 4 | 5 | 6 | 7 |
| 8 | 9 | 10 | 11 | 12 | 13 | 14 |
| 15 | 16 | 17 | 18 | 19 | 20 | 21 |
| 22 | 23 | 24 | 25 | 26 | 27 | 28 |

**Year:** | SOPHOMORE | JUNIOR | SENIOR |

# MONTH
# 5

**APRIL**

| 1 | 2 | 3 | 4 | 5 | 6 | 7 |
|---|---|---|---|---|---|---|
| 8 | 9 | 10 | 11 | 12 | 13 | 14 |
| 15 | 16 | 17 | 18 | 19 | 20 | 21 |
| 22 | 23 | 24 | 25 | 26 | 27 | 28 |

## Year: | SOPHOMORE | JUNIOR | SENIOR

**WHAT** Visit distant colleges

**WHEN** Spring break

**WHY** Actually visiting a college and picturing yourself there is powerful. Having two spring breaks takes pressure off the junior year visit. No matter how extensively you may have read about, talked about, or researched online, the best method is to see colleges in action. Visiting can help eliminate a potential college. Additionally, the admissions office registers that a student has shown interest by visiting. One of the application essays is frequently "Why is this college a match?" This is much easier to write if you have concrete details about the courses and campus.

**HOW** See the separate chapter on "How to do a College Visit" p. 82. Some things to keep in mind:

**Budget at least a half day at each college** Use mapquest and google maps to determine distances.

**Rent a car** unless this is a non-flight trip.

**Take notes** On the form in this book's appendix [or in this book's chapter on visits], use a separate sheet for each college.

**Arrange for lodging** Off campus for your parents, on campus (in a dorm) for yourself

**Take the one hour tour of campus.**

**Complete the information session** and sign the college's paperwork that indicates you came in person.

## A personal note on College Visits

In 25 years of counseling college bound students, very few have transferred from one four-year college to another. Why? Because they spent many months determining the "right" college match in the first place.

# MONTH

# 6

## MAY

| | | | | | | |
|---|---|---|---|---|---|---|
| 1 | 2 | 3 | 4 | 5 | 6 | 7 |
| 8 | 9 | 10 | 11 | 12 | 13 | 14 |
| 15 | 16 | 17 | 18 | 19 | 20 | 21 |
| 22 | 23 | 24 | 25 | 26 | 27 | 28 |

## Year:

| SOPHOMORE | JUNIOR | SENIOR |
|---|---|---|

# MONTH

## 6

**MAY**

| 1 | 2 | 3 | 4 | 5 | 6 | 7 |
|---|---|---|---|---|---|---|
| 8 | 9 | 10 | 11 | 12 | 13 | 14 |
| 15 | 16 | 17 | 18 | 19 | 20 | 21 |
| 22 | 23 | 24 | 25 | 26 | 27 | 28 |

## Year: | SOPHOMORE | JUNIOR | SENIOR |

**WHAT** Advanced Placement (AP) exams

**WHEN** First two weeks of May

**WHY** Colleges recognize that high [a 4 or 5] AP scores are an indication of the ability to do well in college. Your college acceptances can really be enhanced by good AP scores.

**HOW** Use AP prep books. If an exam isn't offered at your school or if you're home schooled, phone **888-225-5427** for locations. **See page 78** to read more on AP testing.

## Effects of AP Exam Scores

If you score at least a 3 on 3 AP exams, you're designated an "AP Scholar." Inversely, scoring a 1 or a 2 can be harmful. See **collegeboard.com** for a complete list of AP awards.

---

## {checklist}

### AND DON'T FORGET

- ☐ Continue SAT prep
- ☐ Continue volunteering
- ☐ Continue to read of and talk about colleges that might be a match.
- ☐ If you haven't done so already, register for the SAT Subject Tests (taken in June) in your current science and history classes.

# MONTH

# 7

## JUNE

| | | | | | | |
|---|---|---|---|---|---|---|
| 1 | 2 | 3 | 4 | 5 | 6 | 7 |
| 8 | 9 | 10 | 11 | 12 | 13 | 14 |
| 15 | 16 | 17 | 18 | 19 | 20 | 21 |
| 22 | 23 | 24 | 25 | 26 | 27 | 28 |

**Year:** | SOPHOMORE | JUNIOR | SENIOR |

# MONTH

## 7

**JUNE**

| 1 | 2 | 3 | 4 | 5 | 6 | 7 |
|---|---|---|---|---|---|---|
| 8 | 9 | 10 | 11 | 12 | 13 | 14 |
| 15 | 16 | 17 | 18 | 19 | 20 | 21 |
| 22 | 23 | 24 | 25 | 26 | 27 | 28 |

## Year: SOPHOMORE | JUNIOR | SENIOR

**WHAT** Confirm the accuracy of sophomore grades.
**WHEN** Mid to late June
**WHY** When they consider candidates for admission, colleges calculate your overall GPA as well as a grid reflecting grades in five "solid" subjects (math, science, history, English, and foreign language). An A in PE doesn't carry the same importance as an A in an Advanced Placement class.
**HOW** If your report card reads differently than you expected, your parent needs to contact the teacher in person immediately (staff leaves during July). If it's appropriate, your parent might question the teacher's documentation of your work. For instance, a teacher might have recorded a test grade inaccurately, or failed to note that you turned in assignments on time. High school staff is generally gone during July, so this must be done in person, in June.

## {checklist}

### AND DON'T FORGET

- ☐ Begin to formulate your college list based on stretch (optimistic) colleges vs. safety (realistic) colleges.
- ☐ Take SAT subject test(s) for which you've registered.

## Write A Grade Change Appeal Letter

Appeals shouldn't be frivolous. You want your appeal to provide the teacher with new information about your case so that he or she can re-evaluate the situation. You might want to explain circumstances such as Illness or death in the family. Also express a willingness to do additional work for extra credit. Send a copy of your appeal letter to the school principal and to your college counselor.

# MONTH

# 8

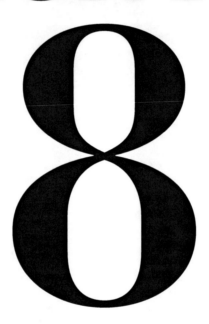

**JULY**

| | | | | | | |
|---|---|---|---|---|---|---|
| 1 | 2 | 3 | 4 | 5 | 6 | 7 |
| 8 | 9 | 10 | 11 | 12 | 13 | 14 |
| 15 | 16 | 17 | 18 | 19 | 20 | 21 |
| 22 | 23 | 24 | 25 | 26 | 27 | 28 |

**Year:** | **SOPHOMORE** | **JUNIOR** | **SENIOR** |

# MONTH

# 8

## JULY

| 1 | 2 | 3 | 4 | 5 | 6 | 7 |
|---|---|---|---|---|---|---|
| 8 | 9 | 10 | 11 | 12 | 13 | 14 |
| 15 | 16 | 17 | 18 | 19 | 20 | 21 |
| 22 | 23 | 24 | 25 | 26 | 27 | 28 |

## Year: | SOPHOMORE | JUNIOR | SENIOR |

**WHAT** Volunteering or internships

**WHEN** June, July and August

**WHY** Without the time commitments of homework, you can devote extra hours to summer "giving back." The days of just working on your tan are over. Colleges want to know how you spend your free time from grades 9 through 12. The level of involvement is more important than the number of activities. As stated in The *500 Best Ways for Teens to Spend the Summer*, "Summer programs are the ace up your sleeve. They are the true point of differentiation for college admissions."

**HOW** Find a program in your interest area. Look for groups that need your expertise. For example, if you love horses, volunteer at a horse camp. If you love Judo, teach it to disadvantaged students.

## Don't Wait to Commit to Volunteer

Dedicate specific hours and specific days to volunteering. If you just wait until you have a few extra hours to devote to a cause, the summer can slip away.

## {checklist}

## AND DON'T FORGET

☐ Make sure you are reading books all summer long! The American Library Association has book lists online. Go to **ala.org/ala/yalsa/booklistsawards/booklistsbook.cfm**. See Month 9 for more details.

# MONTH
# 9

| AUGUST | | | | | | |
|---|---|---|---|---|---|---|
| 1 | 2 | 3 | 4 | 5 | 6 | 7 |
| 8 | 9 | 10 | 11 | 12 | 13 | 14 |
| 15 | 16 | 17 | 18 | 19 | 20 | 21 |
| 22 | 23 | 24 | 25 | 26 | 27 | 28 |

**Year:** | SOPHOMORE | JUNIOR | SENIOR |

# MONTH
# 9

**AUGUST**

| 1 | 2 | 3 | 4 | 5 | 6 | 7 |
|---|---|---|---|---|---|---|
| 8 | 9 | 10 | 11 | 12 | 13 | 14 |
| 15 | 16 | 17 | 18 | 19 | 20 | 21 |
| 22 | 23 | 24 | 25 | 26 | 27 | 28 |

## Year: | SOPHOMORE | **JUNIOR** | SENIOR |

**WHAT** Read! Read! Read! It's important, though, that you read quality literature as well as fun material.

**WHEN** Spend 5-8 hours per week reading, every week throughout **July and August**

**WHY** Your ability to analyze literature (and, as a consequence, to write well) will improve dramatically by actually reading quality literature. This ability will show up as higher test scores and better grades in high school and college.

**HOW** Google reading lists for titles that won the National Book Award and Man-Booker Award.

## Develop a Sense of Good Writing and Keep Examples

Keep index cards handy; when you see an example of good writing, copy it onto a card.

## {checklist}

### AND DON'T FORGET

- ☐ Volunteer regularly throughout the summer. See month 8 for details.
- ☐ Take time to play, relax, and de-stress. The coming months will present challenges.

# MONTH
# 10

## SEPTEMBER

| 1 | 2 | 3 | 4 | 5 | 6 | 7 |
|---|---|---|---|---|---|---|
| 8 | 9 | 10 | 11 | 12 | 13 | 14 |
| 15 | 16 | 17 | 18 | 19 | 20 | 21 |
| 22 | 23 | 24 | 25 | 26 | 27 | 28 |

**Year:** | SOPHOMORE | **JUNIOR** | SENIOR |

# MONTH
# 10

SEPTEMBER

| 1 | 2 | 3 | 4 | 5 | 6 | 7 |
|---|---|---|---|---|---|---|
| 8 | 9 | 10 | 11 | 12 | 13 | 14 |
| 15 | 16 | 17 | 18 | 19 | 20 | 21 |
| 22 | 23 | 24 | 25 | 26 | 27 | 28 |

## Year: SOPHOMORE | **JUNIOR** | SENIOR

**WHAT** Concentrate on getting good grades

**WHEN** Throughout junior year, beginning with the first day of class.

**WHY** Because Early Action/Early Decision methods of application have you apply by November of senior year, colleges won't decide who is admitted early based on senior grades. This means your junior grades are glaringly important. First impressions count.

**HOW** Do all of September's class work, discussions, and homework with an effort of 110%. If later your grades slip due to illness or absences, your teacher will remember your conscientious work and give you a chance to raise your grade.

## {checklist}

### AND DON'T FORGET

- ☐ Register and study for the PSAT
- ☐ Save your graded, analytical papers from classes where you do well to provide to the colleges that request them as part of the application.

## Watch Your Grades

Keep on top of percentages in each class. Many high schools provide on line updates of grades. If your grade by the end of September is lower than 91%, see the teacher to get clarification of areas that need strengthening. There are ways to have these teacher conferences without looking as though you are "grade grubbing." Verbalize it in terms of "What would you, the teacher, analyze as areas for me to work on?"

# MONTH

# 11

## OCTOBER

| 1 | 2 | 3 | 4 | 5 | 6 | 7 |
|---|---|---|---|---|---|---|
| 8 | 9 | 10 | 11 | 12 | 13 | 14 |
| 15 | 16 | 17 | 18 | 19 | 20 | 21 |
| 22 | 23 | 24 | 25 | 26 | 27 | 28 |

**Year:** | SOPHOMORE | JUNIOR | SENIOR |

# MONTH

# 11

## OCTOBER

| 1 | 2 | 3 | 4 | 5 | 6 | 7 |
|---|---|---|---|---|---|---|
| 8 | 9 | 10 | 11 | 12 | 13 | 14 |
| 15 | 16 | 17 | 18 | 19 | 20 | 21 |
| 22 | 23 | 24 | 25 | 26 | 27 | 28 |

**Year:** | SOPHOMORE | **JUNIOR** | SENIOR |

**WHAT** Take the PSAT, a 2 hour exam

**WHEN** During the month of October. Your school will have schedule information.

**WHY** Although PSAT scores are never seen by colleges, if you do well enough, you may qualify for the National Merit Scholarship program. Admissions officers take note of National Merit finalists.

**HOW** Unlike all other College Board exams [SAT I and SAT subject tests], this test is administered at the high school you attend. Contact the counseling office to pay the fee and confirm test date and time. Don't fill out the PSAT student questionnaire, as it is just a marketing tool that will flood you with mail ads.

## Only One Place to Take the PSAT

You cannot register or get results for the PSAT without going through the high school in your district. Even if you are home schooled, you need to make arrangements through your local high school.

## AND DON'T FORGET

☐ Attend college fairs. To find them, google college fairs and your town name.

# MONTH
# 12

## NOVEMBER

| 1 | 2 | 3 | 4 | 5 | 6 | 7 |
|---|---|---|---|---|---|---|
| 8 | 9 | 10 | 11 | 12 | 13 | 14 |
| 15 | 16 | 17 | 18 | 19 | 20 | 21 |
| 22 | 23 | 24 | 25 | 26 | 27 | 28 |

**Year:** | SOPHOMORE | JUNIOR | SENIOR |

# MONTH
# 12

**NOVEMBER**

| 1 | 2 | 3 | 4 | 5 | 6 | 7 |
|---|---|---|---|---|---|---|
| 8 | 9 | 10 | 11 | 12 | 13 | 14 |
| 15 | 16 | 17 | 18 | 19 | 20 | 21 |
| 22 | 23 | 24 | 25 | 26 | 27 | 28 |

## Year: SOPHOMORE  **JUNIOR**  SENIOR

**WHAT** Hold family discussions about college financial or geographic limits

**WHEN** Throughout fall of junior year

**WHY** Families need to communicate restrictions of geography or funding for college now to avoid arguments later.

**HOW** Because you won't know how much scholarship money you'll be getting until April of senior year, you should discuss different financial scenarios. In the 21st century, it's most common for funding to be a combination of parents, scholarships, loans and student jobs.

## Right Time to Take a Closer Look

By this time, you'll have demonstrated that you're willing to do the work and get good grades. You have a better idea of your own potential and the range of colleges where you have a chance of acceptance.

# MONTH
# 13

## DECEMBER

| 1 | 2 | 3 | 4 | 5 | 6 | 7 |
|---|---|---|---|---|---|---|
| 8 | 9 | 10 | 11 | 12 | 13 | 14 |
| 15 | 16 | 17 | 18 | 19 | 20 | 21 |
| 22 | 23 | 24 | 25 | 26 | 27 | 28 |

**Year:** | SOPHOMORE | **JUNIOR** | SENIOR |

# MONTH

# 13

## DECEMBER

| 1 | 2 | 3 | 4 | 5 | 6 | 7 |
|---|---|---|---|---|---|---|
| 8 | 9 | 10 | 11 | 12 | 13 | 14 |
| 15 | 16 | 17 | 18 | 19 | 20 | 21 |
| 22 | 23 | 24 | 25 | 26 | 27 | 28 |

**Year:** SOPHOMORE | **JUNIOR** | SENIOR

**WHAT** Talk with students home from colleges you are considering.

**WHEN** Over the December break

**WHY** Students attending colleges you're considering are good at describing living and learning there.

**HOW** Schools don't usually provide contact information (out of privacy concerns), so you'll need to use your network of friends to get in touch with local students currently attending the colleges you're considering.

## Plan Ahead to Meet with Students During Visits

You can set up meetings with students now so that you can visit them during your campus visits in the spring.

# MONTH
# 13

DECEMBER

| 1 | 2 | 3 | 4 | 5 | 6 | 7 |
|---|---|---|---|---|---|---|
| 8 | 9 | 10 | 11 | 12 | 13 | 14 |
| 15 | 16 | 17 | 18 | 19 | 20 | 21 |
| 22 | 23 | 24 | 25 | 26 | 27 | 28 |

## Year: SOPHOMORE | JUNIOR | SENIOR

**WHAT** Begin planning your spring break college trip. Purchase airline tickets and reserve a rental car.

**WHEN** During free time this month and next

**WHY** You will probably purchase flight tickets in December or January, so it's time to plan the itinerary.

**HOW** Contact colleges by going to their web sites. Most of these sites have a section titled **Undergraduate Admissions**, which is where you can book tours, information sessions, overnights in dorms, and attendance in classes well in advance of your March or April visit.

## Schools Do Take Notice

The admission offices determine who is serious about their college based, in part, on your visit and how you handle the advance preparation.

{checklist}

## AND DON'T FORGET

☐ Continue to research scholarships available to high school students.

# NOTES:

Colleges to visit during spring break:

_____

_____

_____

_____

_____

Reserved tour:

_____

_____

Reserved information session:

_____

_____

Reserved dorm stay:

_____

_____

Reserved class attendance:

_____

_____

# MONTH

# 14

## JANUARY

| | | | | | | |
|---|---|---|---|---|---|---|
| 1 | 2 | 3 | 4 | 5 | 6 | 7 |
| 8 | 9 | 10 | 11 | 12 | 13 | 14 |
| 15 | 16 | 17 | 18 | 19 | 20 | 21 |
| 22 | 23 | 24 | 25 | 26 | 27 | 28 |

**Year:** | SOPHOMORE | **JUNIOR** | SENIOR |

# MONTH
# 14

## JANUARY

| 1 | 2 | 3 | 4 | 5 | 6 | 7 |
|---|---|---|---|---|---|---|
| 8 | 9 | 10 | 11 | 12 | 13 | 14 |
| 15 | 16 | 17 | 18 | 19 | 20 | 21 |
| 22 | 23 | 24 | 25 | 26 | 27 | 28 |

**Year:** | SOPHOMORE | **JUNIOR** | SENIOR |

**WHAT** Test preparation for SAT & ACT

**WHEN** January - February. SAT and ACT for the first time

**WHY** Except for the nearly 1,000 colleges that value high school work to the exclusion of test scores [see fairtest.org for the list of colleges and their rationale], the standardized tests for SAT I, SAT subject tests and ACT are used for admission decisions .

**HOW** Determine your study style:

$ **Save money** If you are sufficiently self-disciplined, do practice tests on your own, using the multitude of prep books in the bookstore. This can be as effective as the expensive prep courses.

$$ **A bit more expensive** Still requiring some self-discipline but affording ease of use, online courses work well. These cost about $70.

$$$ **Much more expensive** Commercial courses such as Kaplan, Princeton Review, or local test prep companies.

## Tests are Still a Part of the Puzzle

Until there is no grade inflation and a uniformity of grades in all 50 states, standardized tests are a part of the decision....not the biggest piece, but a piece, nonetheless.

## THINK ABOUT IT

You can take the ACT and SAT multiple times and usually submit only your best scores. Try it in fall or winter just for the experience, knowing you'll take it again in the spring. See month 17 for details on the ACT.

# MONTH

# 14

| 1 | 2 | 3 | 4 | 5 | 6 | 7 |
|---|---|---|---|---|---|---|
| 8 | 9 | 10 | 11 | 12 | 13 | 14 |
| 15 | 16 | 17 | 18 | 19 | 20 | 21 |
| 22 | 23 | 24 | 25 | 26 | 27 | 28 |

**Year:** | SOPHOMORE | **JUNIOR** | SENIOR |

**WHAT** Register for SAT I and ACT

**WHEN** January. The first SAT or ACT that juniors take is between January and March (unless you chose to take them earlier for practice). SAT subject exams (see Month 16) will be taken in June.

**WHY** Late fees can be costly, and doing a "standby" status will add around $40 to the fees.

**HOW** Go to **collegeboard.com** for both the SAT I and SAT Subject test registration. Go to **ACT.org** to register for the ACT.

## The ACT and Writing

You will be given a choice of taking the ACT with or without writing. We strongly advise taking the ACT with the 30 minute essay, so that it can be an acceptable replacement for the SAT I, which includes a 25 minute essay. To get comparable scores, you must take the ACT with writing.

{checklist}

AND DON'T FORGET

☐ Apply now for summer jobs, internships and/or courses. Try these web sites: **volunteer.gov**, **volunteermatch.com**, **idealist.org**, and **networkforgood.org**

# NOTES:

Registered for ACT with writing:

Date:                                        Time:

Registered for SAT:

Date:                                        Time:

Summer job possibilities:

Summer internship possibilities:

# MONTH

# 15

## FEBRUARY

| 1 | 2 | 3 | 4 | 5 | 6 | 7 |
|---|---|---|---|---|---|---|
| 8 | 9 | 10 | 11 | 12 | 13 | 14 |
| 15 | 16 | 17 | 18 | 19 | 20 | 21 |
| 22 | 23 | 24 | 25 | 26 | 27 | 28 |

**Year:** | SOPHOMORE | **JUNIOR** | SENIOR |

# MONTH
# 15

**FEBRUARY**

| 1 | 2 | 3 | 4 | 5 | 6 | 7 |
|---|---|---|---|---|---|---|
| 8 | 9 | 10 | 11 | 12 | 13 | 14 |
| 15 | 16 | 17 | 18 | 19 | 20 | 21 |
| 22 | 23 | 24 | 25 | 26 | 27 | 28 |

## Year:  SOPHOMORE  **JUNIOR**  SENIOR

**WHAT** Refine your college list to include safety (realistic), midrange (in-between) and stretch (optimistic) schools.

**WHEN** Daily throughout February

**WHY** College tour appointments and classroom attendance must be finalized this month because campus tours tend to fill up quickly over spring break.

**HOW** Take full advantage of the resources available at your school, on the individual college websites, on **collegeprowler.com** and **facebook.com**, and in books such as *The Fiske Guide to Colleges*, *The Yale Insider's Guide*, and *Colleges That Change Lives*.

**Three tips for choosing the right college:**

**1.** Combine colleges that appeal to you (for what they offer and where they're located), with an honest appraisal of your chances of getting in.

**2.** Don't wing it and hope for the best. Consider all your choices carefully—from stretch to safety—and give each college your best possible application. That way, you'll be satisfied regardless of the outcome in spring.

**3.** When you compare colleges, look at their four-year graduation rates (Kiplinger has statistics).

## Save Money and Time

Choosing the right four-year college the first time saves money because it gets you out into the job market a year or more ahead of students who end up transferring because they didn't research the right match.

# MONTH
# 16

## MARCH

| 1 | 2 | 3 | 4 | 5 | 6 | 7 |
|---|---|---|---|---|---|---|
| 8 | 9 | 10 | 11 | 12 | 13 | 14 |
| 15 | 16 | 17 | 18 | 19 | 20 | 21 |
| 22 | 23 | 24 | 25 | 26 | 27 | 28 |

**Year:** SOPHOMORE    JUNIOR    SENIOR

# MONTH
# 16

## MARCH

| 1 | 2 | 3 | 4 | 5 | 6 | 7 |
|---|---|---|---|---|---|---|
| 8 | 9 | 10 | 11 | 12 | 13 | 14 |
| 15 | 16 | 17 | 18 | 19 | 20 | 21 |
| 22 | 23 | 24 | 25 | 26 | 27 | 28 |

## Year: SOPHOMORE **JUNIOR** SENIOR

**WHAT** Take the SAT again.

**WHEN** Between March and May (you can also take the ACT again now or at the end of junior year).

**WHY** Some colleges still look at all SAT scores, but many allow you to submit your highest score from one test date only.

**HOW** Arrive at test center early. Bring snacks and a watch; you won't be allowed to use your cell phone as a timepiece. The first item is the 25 minute essay. Notice carefully the start time, write it down and record the time 25 minutes later. Some proctors stop students at 23 minutes and you must speak up if you have been given less than the allotted 25 minutes. Bring a calculator.

## You Can Avoid Multiple Tests

If you prepare ahead, you can avoid the added stress of taking this long exam more than twice. See p. 76 on Preparing for Standardized Tests.

## {checklist}

### AND DON'T FORGET

☐ Make sure you are registered for the first ACT test (to be taken in February) at **act.org**.

# MONTH
# 17

**APRIL**

|  |  |  |  |  |  |  |
|---|---|---|---|---|---|---|
| 1 | 2 | 3 | 4 | 5 | 6 | 7 |
| 8 | 9 | 10 | 11 | 12 | 13 | 14 |
| 15 | 16 | 17 | 18 | 19 | 20 | 21 |
| 22 | 23 | 24 | 25 | 26 | 27 | 28 |

**Year:** | SOPHOMORE | JUNIOR | SENIOR |

# MONTH

# 17

**APRIL**

| 1 | 2 | 3 | 4 | 5 | 6 | 7 |
|---|---|---|---|---|---|---|
| 8 | 9 | 10 | 11 | 12 | 13 | 14 |
| 15 | 16 | 17 | 18 | 19 | 20 | 21 |
| 22 | 23 | 24 | 25 | 26 | 27 | 28 |

## Year: SOPHOMORE | **JUNIOR** | SENIOR

**WHAT** Take the ACT with writing again.

**WHEN** April

**WHY** A student can select ACT scores from one test day only, hiding all other attempts. For this reason, a student might take the ACT as early as fall of junior year, or more than twice.

**HOW** Make certain you take the ACT with the optional writing section each time. Only with that writing portion can the ACT replace the SAT I and sometimes the SAT Subject tests as well.

## Advantages of the ACT

There is no penalty for guessing, there are only four answers to choose from (as opposed to SAT's five), all scores but one can be hidden from colleges, and it's nearly an hour shorter than the SAT.

## {checklist}

### AND DON'T FORGET

- ☐ Register at **collegeboard.com** for 2 SAT subject tests to be taken in June. **Pick and register for your two strongest subjects.**
- ☐ Buy a prep book for the SAT subject tests you chose.
- ☐ Register for the second ACT.

# MONTH

# 17

## APRIL

| 1 | 2 | 3 | 4 | 5 | 6 | 7 |
|---|---|---|---|---|---|---|
| 8 | 9 | 10 | 11 | 12 | 13 | 14 |
| 15 | 16 | 17 | 18 | 19 | 20 | 21 |
| 22 | 23 | 24 | 25 | 26 | 27 | 28 |

**Year:** | SOPHOMORE | **JUNIOR** | SENIOR |

**WHAT** Visit the more distant colleges on your list.
**WHEN** During spring break—rarely the same time as the colleges' break—you'll see colleges while they are in session.
**WHY** There's nothing like seeing a campus for yourself. This will be your home for four years, so take the time to carefully test drive it.
**HOW** Make certain to sign all cards and sign-in sheets that the admissions office provides. These become part of your application. Take notes for each college visit, and try to limit your visits to a total of two colleges per day. If you travel far from home, you will want to use between three and eight days to see colleges in the larger general area. For example, colleges in and around Boston, New York, Philadelphia and Washington D.C. can be seen in one trip.
**See page 82** for more about visiting colleges.

## Show How Serious You Are

Certainly, this message can be conveyed by an Early Decision application, but, short of that, a visit helps the admissions office believe in a candidate's seriousness.

# NOTES:

My impression of colleges visited:

**College name:**

Academics:

Social:

Housing guaranteed all 4 years?

**College name:**

Academics:

Social:

Housing guaranteed all 4 years?

**College name:**

Academics:

Social:

Housing guaranteed all 4 years?

**College name:**

Academics:

Social:

Housing guaranteed all 4 years?

# MONTH

# 18

## MAY

| | | | | | | |
|---|---|---|---|---|---|---|
| 1 | 2 | 3 | 4 | 5 | 6 | 7 |
| 8 | 9 | 10 | 11 | 12 | 13 | 14 |
| 15 | 16 | 17 | 18 | 19 | 20 | 21 |
| 22 | 23 | 24 | 25 | 26 | 27 | 28 |

**Year:** | SOPHOMORE | **JUNIOR** | SENIOR |

# MONTH
# 18

MAY

| 1 | 2 | 3 | 4 | 5 | 6 | 7 |
| 8 | 9 | 10 | 11 | 12 | 13 | 14 |
| 15 | 16 | 17 | 18 | 19 | 20 | 21 |
| 22 | 23 | 24 | 25 | 26 | 27 | 28 |

## Year: SOPHOMORE | **JUNIOR** | SENIOR

**WHAT** Visit nearby colleges

**WHEN** Over the long Memorial Day weekend

**WHY** Don't eliminate a college just because it's close by. Although getting away from home can yield additional "life learnings," nearby colleges can be good match schools.

**HOW** <u>See our guidelines about visiting colleges on</u> <u>page 82.</u>

## Getting the Real College Experience Near Home

As long as you live on campus, you'll get the college experience even if it is only a short distance from home. You can change your college "geography" without going thousands of miles away.

# MONTH
# 18

## MAY

| 1 | 2 | 3 | 4 | 5 | 6 | 7 |
|---|---|---|---|---|---|---|
| 8 | 9 | 10 | 11 | 12 | 13 | 14 |
| 15 | 16 | 17 | 18 | 19 | 20 | 21 |
| 22 | 23 | 24 | 25 | 26 | 27 | 28 |

## Year: SOPHOMORE | **JUNIOR** | SENIOR

**WHAT** Get teacher recommendations

**WHEN** May, early June

**WHY** Teachers change schools. Teachers retire. Catch them now while they are around. Recommendations by teachers are looked at closely by schools, and can often make the difference when a college is faced with many similar applicants.

**HOW**
- Go to **commonapp.org**
- Download teacher recommendation form
- Mark 'yes' in the box that indicates that you waive the right to see the recommendation.
- Give form plus brag sheet (see Month 22) to teacher

Teacher will ask: "Where do you want me to send it?"
Your answer: "You can keep it until I know specific colleges or you can give it to me to mail next October."

## Dig Up the Saved Papers

Help your teachers write the best recommendations possible by providing copies of the good analytical papers you've been saving up all year to show to the colleges who may request them. These will enable your teachers to accurately remember your strong areas.

# NOTES:

Teachers recommendation requests:

Teacher #1. _____ Checked back with on: _____

Teacher #2. _____ Checked back with on: _____


Thank you card/gift to both teachers on:

_____

# MONTH

# 19

## JUNE

| 1 | 2 | 3 | 4 | 5 | 6 | 7 |
|---|---|---|---|---|---|---|
| 8 | 9 | 10 | 11 | 12 | 13 | 14 |
| 15 | 16 | 17 | 18 | 19 | 20 | 21 |
| 22 | 23 | 24 | 25 | 26 | 27 | 28 |

**Year:** | SOPHOMORE | **JUNIOR** | SENIOR |

# MONTH
# 19

**JUNE**

| 1 | 2 | 3 | 4 | 5 | 6 | 7 |
|---|---|---|---|---|---|---|
| 8 | 9 | 10 | 11 | 12 | 13 | 14 |
| 15 | 16 | 17 | 18 | 19 | 20 | 21 |
| 22 | 23 | 24 | 25 | 26 | 27 | 28 |

**Year:** | SOPHOMORE | **JUNIOR** | SENIOR |

**WHAT** Continue to evaluate your list of colleges.

**WHEN** All summer

**WHY** Your ideas about the best college environment are constantly evolving. Your college ideas might be very different from when you began this process in Month 1.

**HOW** Get very introspective. Several of the colleges on the original list have now been visited, complete with college class attendance during the sophomore and junior year spring breaks. Make certain that you have a mix of colleges, from safety schools to highly competitive admissions schools. Generally, you should have a total of 8-10 schools whose acceptance rates range from 10% to 70%. <u>Use the College Comparison Chart on **page 74.**</u>

## Be Open to Changing the List

Examine how you learn best and then eliminate colleges from your original list that no longer fit. Add any colleges that now seem to fit because of college visits, new research or recent suggestions from students or teachers.

# MONTH
# 19

## JUNE

| 1 | 2 | 3 | 4 | 5 | 6 | 7 |
|---|---|---|---|---|---|---|
| 8 | 9 | 10 | 11 | 12 | 13 | 14 |
| 15 | 16 | 17 | 18 | 19 | 20 | 21 |
| 22 | 23 | 24 | 25 | 26 | 27 | 28 |

## Year: SOPHOMORE | **JUNIOR** | SENIOR

**WHAT** Involve yourself in summer volunteering.

**WHEN** Throughout the summer, minimum six hours per week.

**WHY** Volunteering demonstrates your interests, your strengths and your inclination to give back to the community. Often, these activities become the topic of your short and long college essays. Colleges look for more than just good grades. They want to see if you are contributing to the world.

**HOW** Keep a record of the hours you spend. Keep a journal of what challenged you and what you enjoyed about it.

## What It Says About You

When you volunteer, especially for something that makes sense in terms of your interests, colleges believe you will continue to contribute to the world at large as well as to their campuses specifically.

# MONTH
# 19

JUNE

| 1 | 2 | 3 | 4 | 5 | 6 | 7 |
|---|---|---|---|---|---|---|
| 8 | 9 | 10 | 11 | 12 | 13 | 14 |
| 15 | 16 | 17 | 18 | 19 | 20 | 21 |
| 22 | 23 | 24 | 25 | 26 | 27 | 28 |

## Year: SOPHOMORE | JUNIOR | SENIOR

**WHAT** Take two SAT subject tests. These are one hour, multiple choice exams on specific subjects.

**WHEN** June SAT date

**WHY** Most colleges recommend (and some require) two good SAT Subject scores. Some colleges even expect three. It's best to take these tests when the material is fresh.

**HOW** Continue to take several timed practice tests from the books you've worked in since April.

## Last Minute Change of Mind

If you registered in April for a subject and now feel stronger in a different one, you can change the subject you take as late as the moment you walk in.

# MONTH
# 19

## JUNE

| 1 | 2 | 3 | 4 | 5 | 6 | 7 |
|---|---|---|---|---|---|---|
| 8 | 9 | 10 | 11 | 12 | 13 | 14 |
| 15 | 16 | 17 | 18 | 19 | 20 | 21 |
| 22 | 23 | 24 | 25 | 26 | 27 | 28 |

## Year:   SOPHOMORE   **JUNIOR**   SENIOR

**WHAT** Take the ACT with writing again.

**WHEN** Mid-June

**WHY** Nearly all colleges accept the ACT as a replacement for the SAT I. Also, because the ACT is very subject-based, it can often replace an SAT subject test.

**HOW** Look over your first ACT score sheet. Focus on practicing in areas where you can gain the most points.

**NOTE:** The ACT system makes it harder to qualify for LD (learning disability) accommodations than does the SAT system. So if you have a disability or need extra time to complete the test, you must document your requirements with a psychologist several months ahead.

## The Difference a Second Chance Can Make

If you have a score around 27, this indicates that you have certain strengths. By repeating the exam, it is not uncommon to raise your score 3 points. The highest possible ACT score is 36, and a very good score is around 31. Three points can make a big difference!

## {checklist}

### AND DON'T FORGET

- ☐ Continue volunteering
- ☐ Start some summer reading
- ☐ Research scholarships on your high school's website and on **fastweb.com** and **finaid.com**. Continue this for the next 11 months.

# NOTES:

Summer reading completed:

Deadlines for Scholarships to apply for:

Scholarship announcement dates:

# MONTH
# 20

## JULY

| 1 | 2 | 3 | 4 | 5 | 6 | 7 |
|---|---|---|---|---|---|---|
| 8 | 9 | 10 | 11 | 12 | 13 | 14 |
| 15 | 16 | 17 | 18 | 19 | 20 | 21 |
| 22 | 23 | 24 | 25 | 26 | 27 | 28 |

**Year:** SOPHOMORE **JUNIOR** SENIOR

# MONTH
# 20

**JULY**

| 1 | 2 | 3 | 4 | 5 | 6 | 7 |
|---|---|---|---|---|---|---|
| 8 | 9 | 10 | 11 | 12 | 13 | 14 |
| 15 | 16 | 17 | 18 | 19 | 20 | 21 |
| 22 | 23 | 24 | 25 | 26 | 27 | 28 |

## Year: SOPHOMORE **JUNIOR** SENIOR

**WHAT** Write the first drafts of your personal essays.
**WHEN** July, August and polished by the end of August
**WHY** There is much to lose by procrastinating and little to gain by waiting! The quality of essays is improved by writing them during the summer and doing multiple edits.
**HOW** First, determine if the college accepts the Common Application. Over 400 colleges do, and there is usually a very general essay topic that allows a student to respond with current knowledge and experience. If your college doesn't accept the common application and their web site doesn't yet have this year's essay topics, use any of the common application essay topics.

### Seven tips for the main personal essay:
**1.** Begin by jotting down favorite activities and books.
**2.** Brainstorm with a parent or friend about which activity captures on paper traits you are proud of.
**3.** Take your third draft to an adult who is a good writer.
**4.** Make certain that you are clear about word count required by each college.
**5.** Do re-writes, generally 5-8 of them, with the adult writer checking each version.
**6.** Remember: colleges expect carefully written essays. They know that you have asked a teacher or friend for feedback.

## Common Applications Sometimes Allow for Creativity
For many years, one of the topics on the Common Application has always been "A topic of your choice".

# MONTH
# 21

## AUGUST

| | | | | | | |
|---|---|---|---|---|---|---|
| 1 | 2 | 3 | 4 | 5 | 6 | 7 |
| 8 | 9 | 10 | 11 | 12 | 13 | 14 |
| 15 | 16 | 17 | 18 | 19 | 20 | 21 |
| 22 | 23 | 24 | 25 | 26 | 27 | 28 |

**Year:** | SOPHOMORE | **JUNIOR** | SENIOR |

# MONTH
# 21

## AUGUST

| 1 | 2 | 3 | 4 | 5 | 6 | 7 |
|---|---|---|---|---|---|---|
| 8 | 9 | 10 | 11 | 12 | 13 | 14 |
| 15 | 16 | 17 | 18 | 19 | 20 | 21 |
| 22 | 23 | 24 | 25 | 26 | 27 | 28 |

**Year:** | SOPHOMORE | JUNIOR | **SENIOR** |

**WHAT** Write the short essays (sometimes called supplemental essays) required by many Common and non-common Application colleges.

**WHEN** Complete by the end of September

**WHY** These essays capture other strong traits; they are sometimes limited to 100 words. (Topics are straightforward: describe yourself; write a note to your roommate, why [name of college] is a good match college for you, what high school subject you liked most.) You know as much about your traits now as you will in two months, so complete these before school starts.

**HOW** Make a list of all topics required by all colleges. (They are listed on each college's web site under the highlighted section "Undergraduate Admissions". There is no charge for this information.) Print out all prompts for each essay. Look for overlaps by lining up all prompts, stacking the common topics in one pile.

## Make It Easier

Even though you may apply to ten colleges with dozens of potential supplemental essays, you will probably only need to write four or five essays (in addition to the one main essay) if you pay attention to overlapping prompts.

# MONTH

# 22

## SEPTEMBER

|    |    |    |    |    |    |    |
|----|----|----|----|----|----|----|
| 1  | 2  | 3  | 4  | 5  | 6  | 7  |
| 8  | 9  | 10 | 11 | 12 | 13 | 14 |
| 15 | 16 | 17 | 18 | 19 | 20 | 21 |
| 22 | 23 | 24 | 25 | 26 | 27 | 28 |

**Year:** | SOPHOMORE | JUNIOR | **SENIOR** |

# MONTH

# 22

**SEPTEMBER**

| 1 | 2 | 3 | 4 | 5 | 6 | 7 |
|---|---|---|---|---|---|---|
| 8 | 9 | 10 | 11 | 12 | 13 | 14 |
| 15 | 16 | 17 | 18 | 19 | 20 | 21 |
| 22 | 23 | 24 | 25 | 26 | 27 | 28 |

**Year:** | SOPHOMORE | JUNIOR | **SENIOR** |

**WHAT** Ask for teacher recommendations. Write a one-page outside the classroom resumé and a one-page inside the classroom resumé.

**WHEN** Early in the school year, by late September at the latest.

**WHY** To remind teachers of who you are (inside and outside the classroom) when you ask for their recommendations. Colleges have many students with similar grades and similar test scores. Admissions officers often use teacher opinions as a way to distinguish your classroom behavior and eagerness to learn.

**HOW** Your first one-page sheet should describe what you have done outside the classroom—this will look much like a formal resumé. On another sheet, write a description of what you have done well in that teacher's class. The more detailed you can be, the better the recommendation. Refer to a project or a class discussion that your teacher can address in the recommendation. **See page 77** for an example of an outside the classroom resumé.

NOTE: Each high school has its own procedure for sending counselor and teacher recommendations. Increasingly, these are sent electronically, allowing you to skip the envelope step. Check with your high school counselor.

## What to Expect

Each college has its own procedure for teacher recommendations. For example, the Common Application offers an electronic teacher recommendation form, but non-Common App colleges use their own forms. Generally, you give each teacher your two resumés, the college's form, and a stamped envelope addressed to each college. You do this for every college, so you might be handing a teacher ten envelopes!

.

# MONTH
# 23

## OCTOBER

|  |  |  |  |  |  |  |
|---|---|---|---|---|---|---|
| 1 | 2 | 3 | 4 | 5 | 6 | 7 |
| 8 | 9 | 10 | 11 | 12 | 13 | 14 |
| 15 | 16 | 17 | 18 | 19 | 20 | 21 |
| 22 | 23 | 24 | 25 | 26 | 27 | 28 |

**Year:** | SOPHOMORE | JUNIOR | SENIOR |

# MONTH

# 23

## OCTOBER

| 1 | 2 | 3 | 4 | 5 | 6 | 7 |
|---|---|---|---|---|---|---|
| 8 | 9 | 10 | 11 | 12 | 13 | 14 |
| 15 | 16 | 17 | 18 | 19 | 20 | 21 |
| 22 | 23 | 24 | 25 | 26 | 27 | 28 |

## Year: SOPHOMORE | JUNIOR | **SENIOR**

**WHAT** Complete all Early Action or Early Decision applications.

**WHEN** By November 1

**WHY** A strategy that includes application for early admission almost always increases your likelihood of acceptance, sometimes doubling your odds. We don't have to mention what a relief it is to know you've been accepted by December 15th of your senior year, instead of normal acceptance announcements that arrive in April.

**HOW** Complete all unfilled portions of the application, such as the activities and awards sections. Provide all teachers and counselors who are writing recommendations with your resumés and appropriate forms. Two weeks before the real due date, write thank you cards to the teachers and counselors who wrote your recommendations. **See page 80 for more on Early Action/Early Decision.**

NOTE: It's rare, but some colleges offer rolling admissions programs. If your college offers this option, do these applications first, by early October.

## New Counselor?

Don't know your counselor as well as you know the principal? The counselor form (Secondary School Report) can be filled out by the counselor or any high school administrator.

.

## {checklist}

### AND DON'T FORGET

☐ Send SAT and ACT scores to colleges. These must be received by November for Early Action/Early Decision. Go to **collegeboard.com** or **act.org**.

# MONTH

# 24

## NOVEMBER

| | | | | | | |
|---|---|---|---|---|---|---|
| 1 | 2 | 3 | 4 | 5 | 6 | 7 |
| 8 | 9 | 10 | 11 | 12 | 13 | 14 |
| 15 | 16 | 17 | 18 | 19 | 20 | 21 |
| 22 | 23 | 24 | 25 | 26 | 27 | 28 |

**Year:** | SOPHOMORE | JUNIOR | **SENIOR** |

# MONTH
# 24

## NOVEMBER

| 1 | 2 | 3 | 4 | 5 | 6 | 7 |
|---|---|---|---|---|---|---|
| 8 | 9 | 10 | 11 | 12 | 13 | 14 |
| 15 | 16 | 17 | 18 | 19 | 20 | 21 |
| 22 | 23 | 24 | 25 | 26 | 27 | 28 |

## Year: | SOPHOMORE | JUNIOR | SENIOR |

**WHAT** Set up interviews with college admissions personnel or college alumni.

**WHEN** Early November

**WHY** Interviews show enthusiasm for the college and show self-organization and initiative.
Additionally, you can get questions answered specific to that college.

**HOW** Prepare for the interviews by talking with college students and with adults. <u>**See page 86** for the article on interviews.</u>

## Scheduling an Interview

1. Plan two to three weeks ahead.
2. Ask for a confirmation by e-mail and bring your transcript and resumé.
3. To be fresh for the interview, schedule it before the tour.

# MONTH

# 25

## DECEMBER

| 1 | 2 | 3 | 4 | 5 | 6 | 7 |
|---|---|---|---|---|---|---|
| 8 | 9 | 10 | 11 | 12 | 13 | 14 |
| 15 | 16 | 17 | 18 | 19 | 20 | 21 |
| 22 | 23 | 24 | 25 | 26 | 27 | 28 |

**Year:** | SOPHOMORE | JUNIOR | **SENIOR** |

# MONTH
# 25

**DECEMBER**

| 1 | 2 | 3 | 4 | 5 | 6 | 7 |
| 8 | 9 | 10 | 11 | 12 | 13 | 14 |
| 15 | 16 | 17 | 18 | 19 | 20 | 21 |
| 22 | 23 | 24 | 25 | 26 | 27 | 28 |

## Year: | SOPHOMORE | JUNIOR | **SENIOR** |

**WHAT** Continue researching scholarships (see fastweb.com and finaid.com), with a focus on local scholarships. It can work well to find scholarships requiring an essay.

**WHEN** Through the end of senior year

**WHY** Scholarships can lighten the financial burden significantly. Even a small one can cover books for a college year. The rationale for applying for local scholarships is that the competition is less intense than for national scholarships.

**HOW** By applying for scholarships requiring an essay, you will have less competition. You will already have written good essays about your individual interests and strengths and these polished essays can help you in this other pursuit: getting money for college.

## Scholarships Can Do More Than You Think

In some cases, being awarded a scholarship before you enter a college can help to make you more likely to get another one during college. Also, you can list scholarships on your application (under the awards section), or when you are looking for a job.

# ADDITIONAL RESOURCES

# ADDITIONAL RESOURCES

## SELF ASSESSMENT SURVEY

There's nothing harder for most adolescents than to describe their personal preferences. You can enjoy pizzas and burgers, after all. But you probably can describe some aspects of your personality. Are you outgoing or shy? Organized or scattered? Would you rather be coached through a new experience or discover things on your own?

The attributes that follow don't have "right" answers, and it's entirely possible that you will answer them differently a year from now. Just remember, there are over 3,000 four-year colleges in the United States, which means you have a lot of choices.

To help you decide where you'll learn the most and fit in the best, it helps to divide colleges into a few basic categories. Don't look at costs, at least not at the exploratory stage. This is the time to explore the world of higher education!

Eventually, though, you'll need to look at colleges in relation to your own preferences. Not necessarily what your parents want, but where you feel that you'll fit in.

In no particular order, we'll look at Location, Size, Academics, and Extracurricular Activities. Think about your preferences when it comes to each of these choices.

### LOCATION
Distance from home (close, far, or in-between)
Climate (warm, cool)
Campus (urban or small-town; proximity to nature or to city life)
Specific city or state (proximity to relatives, ski slopes, beaches)

### SIZE
Campus life (do you want to be "anonymous" or prominent)
Faculty (well known? approachable?)
Housing options (on-campus? off-campus?)

# ADDITIONAL
# RESOURCES

**ACADEMICS**
Is academic prestige important?
Do you want bright, talented classmates?

**CLASS SIZE (INTIMATE OR LARGER)**
Diversity of student body
Intensity of scholarship

**ACTIVITIES**
Fraternity/Sorority
Athletics?
Male/Female ratio

**RANGE OF OPTIONS FOR OUTSIDE INTERESTS**
To see which colleges might match your preferences, use the Fiske Guide to Colleges as well as college web sites. Then use the chart on **page 74** to compare colleges.

# ADDITIONAL RESOURCES

## COLLEGE COMPARISON CHART

|  | COLLEGE 1 | COLLEGE 2 | COLLEGE 3 | COLLEGE 4 | COLLEGE 5 |  |
|---|---|---|---|---|---|---|
| Percent of students accepted each year |  |  |  |  |  |  |
| Percent of students who return year 2 |  |  |  |  |  |  |
| Professors who care |  |  |  |  |  |  |
| Academically challenging |  |  |  |  |  |  |
| Good dept. in my area of interest |  |  |  |  |  |  |
| Located near home |  |  |  |  |  |  |
| Located away from home |  |  |  |  |  |  |
| Male/female ratio |  |  |  |  |  |  |
| Social environment |  |  |  |  |  |  |
| Study Abroad program |  |  |  |  |  |  |
| Small sized school |  |  |  |  |  |  |
| Large sized school |  |  |  |  |  |  |

# ADDITIONAL
# RESOURCES

Fill in college names, and rate all areas (on a scale of 1 to 10).

| COLLEGE 6 | COLLEGE 7 | COLLEGE 8 | COLLEGE 9 | COLLEGE 10 | COLLEGE 11 | COLLEGE 12 |
|---|---|---|---|---|---|---|
|  |  |  |  |  |  |  |
|  |  |  |  |  |  |  |
|  |  |  |  |  |  |  |
|  |  |  |  |  |  |  |
|  |  |  |  |  |  |  |
|  |  |  |  |  |  |  |
|  |  |  |  |  |  |  |
|  |  |  |  |  |  |  |
|  |  |  |  |  |  |  |
|  |  |  |  |  |  |  |
|  |  |  |  |  |  |  |

# ADDITIONAL RESOURCES

## PREPARING FOR STANDARDIZED TESTS

There's no one-type-fits-all method of studying for SATs and other standardized tests. Think about and look for the best SAT prep method to match your style. For math and major test drills, every student has a different trajectory and personality. I recommend one of three methods to prepare:

• A commercial course offered in the community
• An online course
• An individualized program in which student works through test prep materials.

To put standardized tests in perspective, remember that colleges weigh the high school curriculum most heavily, standardized tests much less so. Though most discussion revolves around the SAT and ACT tests, over 400 excellent four-year colleges don't require any test scores.

# ADDITIONAL RESOURCES

## RECOMMENDATIONS RESUMÉ

Before requesting a recommendation from teachers and counselors, determine whether they will be using electronic or paper submissions. Provide a description, like a resumé to your recommenders. Format your resumé similar to this example:

**Your name**
**Your phone number**
**Your email address**

**Academic Record**
    Grade point average
    List of advanced courses
    SAT and/or ACT scores

**Extracurricular Activities**
    Activity name and years involved
    Role you played
    Service you provided

**School Activities**
    Name of activity and years involved
    [For Example] school newspaper, grade 9 submitted articles, grade 11 editor

**Awards and Honors**
    Name of award and when awarded
    Explanation of the award or honor

In addition to this resumé [AKA Brag Sheet], you will be giving to teachers and counselors these materials:

- A short paragraph thanking him/her for writing the recommendation
- A one page resumé of outstanding class contributions or projects
- A short paragraph asking that your outstanding project or discussions be mentioned.
- The recommendation form from individual colleges if your school does not submit forms electronically.
- A list of colleges you are applying to.
- Stamped, addressed envelopes for each college if your school does not submit forms electronically.

# ADDITIONAL RESOURCES

# No Fear AP Testing

BY AMY BOBEDA, EDITORIAL INTERN AND COLLEGE STUDENT

Advanced Placement classes resemble the ultimate horror film. My first AP class made me long to trade places with Drew Barrymore in *Scream*. Phone stalkers and ax murderers seemed far more appealing than stressing over presidents, monopolies, and Watergate. But, somewhere between JFK and Reganomics the secret to AP success was revealed: just study.

While the concept seemed utterly obvious, AP classes are highly structured, with the College Board nit-picking random facts from the universe of textbook knowledge. At first, I had no idea where to begin.

AP classes can be split into two goals: first, to pass the class, then to pass the test.

While most high school classes have curriculum structured around quizzes, tests, and finals, the same is not true in AP classes. Students can ace their AP classes but score a 2 (a terrible mark, since the top AP score is a 5) on the exam or visa versa. If a teacher grades easily, students may not be prepared for the test. Every class has a different teacher, most have different texts, and not all classes are taught to maximize success on the AP test that follows.

To succeed in the AP classroom, strategies are as varied as teachers. Treat it like any other class, but know that the teacher expects more. You're going to have to do the work, read the book, participate in study groups, and pay attention. If you take the initiative to enroll in an AP class, hoping to help your chances for college admission or to boost your GPA, you should be willing to put in a little more effort when a teacher demands it.

Passing the test, however, can be approached differently.

The best bet to taking down the beast is to invest in study guides for every AP class. Every company that makes guides for the SAT and ACT also offers guides for AP tests. Get a few for each subject as each book is structured differently. Princeton Review books are usually in paragraph form, while Kaplan gives little snippits of information. Each book varies somewhat on their content, which can help one cover all the bases, but the real key is to know the information that overlaps. If three AP Economics books have a section on Phillips Curves, there is a pretty good chance the AP test will ask for a drawing of a Phillips Curve. The

# ADDITIONAL
# RESOURCES

folks who publish a new edition of an AP study guide every year do, in fact, take the time to study AP test trends and have a pretty accurate idea of what to expect on free response and multiple-choice questions.

(If the piggy bank doesn't allow for the investment, check out the local library, chances are they may have a few copies, or share review books with classmates. Also, consider the Internet and AP teachers as valuable resources. Every four years an AP test is released to the public, every AP student should get some and take them. As usual, practice makes perfect.)

As for a studying timeframe, obviously it varies by student. Some like to review the first semester's curriculum over winter break. Others wait a little longer. I'd recommend waiting until a month or so before the test—spring break is usually a great time to crack open the books—but you have to consider how many other tests are on your docket, and how you truly feel about their chances of success in each subject.

Studying strategies are pretty basic: group study or solitary study. I suggest trying both, and seeing what works best. Often teachers will hold study groups during free periods, after school, or lunch. Once, I had an AP teacher who would feed us pizza if we came to study group. They are often a convenient way to de-stress about the test and study simultaneously.

Strategy is key; you must learn how to play the testing game. The answers are not what the student believes, but rather, what the College Board believes. Know the rules: wrong answers deduct a fraction of a point on multiple-choice questions, but impose no penalty on free responses. Know the time limits. Have confidence that the test will end in your favor.

Lastly, remember that the test is not a test from the textbook. Hundreds of paragraphs will be totally irrelevant on the AP test, so reviewing the book in depth is often an inefficient use of your time.

Hopefully, these strategies and insight can help any AP student escape the fate of Drew Barrymore, and instead, like Neve Campbell, defeat the mass murderer and pass the oh-so-terrifying AP test.

On a side note: consider taking SAT 2 subject tests in the subjects you have AP tested in. For example if you take AP US History, try taking the US History SAT 2 when it is offered in May or June. It will either fall right before the AP test and provide some excellent last minute review, or will occur right after the AP test when everything is fresh in your brain.

# ADDITIONAL RESOURCES

## EARLY ACTION AND EARLY DECISION

Early Action and Early Decision plans have specific application deadlines, generally two months before regular applications are due. Senior first semester grades will not be seen by colleges before they offer admission, so junior year grades are very important when applying early.

Why rush this final step in the application process?

Students almost always have a better chance of admission if applying in the early group. Even Ivy League schools accept a higher percentage [often double] of early applicants and are filling a large share of classes from the early pool. Additionally, this early effort saves students psychologically by avoiding the nail-biting, five-month wait to find out from regular admit colleges in April.

Early Action does not mean that you have to commit to attend if you are accepted in December. That decision, like that of regular applications, can be made as late as May 1 of senior year. You may continue to apply to other colleges.

Early Decision, on the other hand, is binding, meaning you must attend that school and, if accepted, withdraw all other applications in December. Your reward: nearly twice the chance of acceptance.

(Note that there's a third category called Rolling Admissions. This is fairly rare. It's a "First Come, First Admitted" method, often filling the class long before the actual posted deadline.)

# ADDITIONAL
# RESOURCES

An important clarification: After a heated debate back in 2001, the National Association of College Admissions Counselors got the colleges to agree to the following:

While you may apply to only one school for Early Decision, you can simultaneously apply Rolling or Early Action to others schools. Additionally, you can apply to all colleges that offer Early Action, even if you are applying to one school Early Decision.

One small distinction is made by a few competitive colleges: Single Action Early Action. This program allows for only one Early Action application, in addition to one Early Decision application.

Confused? Phone the admissions office at the school you are considering to find out their policy. These policies are frequently changed, so make that phone call to clarify. On occasion, the phone person will not know, so work hard to confirm, as agreed upon, that you may apply without restrictions using multiple Early Action and one Early Decision.

So, what happens if you are not accepted in December as an early applicant? Again, you will need to ask individual colleges, as some defer your application, putting you in the general pool of applicants who apply regular decision, while others say a denial of admissions in December is final.

# ADDITIONAL RESOURCES

## CAMPUS VISITS: CULTURAL ANTHROPOLOGY

Amber M. had finally made it to her dream school, Amherst, in the rolling hills of western Massachusetts. But as she stood beneath the elm trees and looked across the grassy quadrangle at the brick dormitory, classroom buildings and ivy-covered library where she had imagined spending the next four years, she realized something was wrong. The campus didn't feel right to her: too isolated, too small, too picture-postcard-perfect. Perfect for someone else, no doubt, but wrong for her. She turned to her parents, tears in her eyes, and confessed: Amherst, she told them, wasn't her dream school after all.

The story has a happy ending, though. Amber, whom I'd coached through the college admissions process, hadn't actually enrolled at Amherst, she was just visiting over her spring break. And she'd also been accepted at Wellesley, where she's now a senior. "I'm so happy we made those college visits before I graduated from high school," Amber told me last month.

The American dream of getting into a good college doesn't happen automatically, doesn't become reality without planning, without coaching, without work in the classroom, at home...and on the road.

Families head out over spring break to scout far-off campuses and see for themselves if the buildings, quadrangles and lecture halls match up with the glossy college brochures and fancy university websites. To see for themselves, to "taste with their feet."

But before you take off, I recommend you do a bit of homework. The first step is to set up an itinerary. While you might be tempted just to whip out a map and wing it, consider asking the admissions office for a suggested route between colleges. And don't be surprised if you see the O'Briens from Omaha, the McDonalds from Memphis and the Cohens from Chicago traveling the same campus circuit. Think of yourself as an anthropologist on a research expedition. Clipboard in hand, you're looking for clues to the campus culture. Watch and listen carefully, take plenty of notes and pictures. As any scientist will tell you, visual memories blur quickly if you don't record your observations. Note how the students dress; listen in to their conversations. Are they talking about courses or cars? Politics or parties? Does the campus mood seem cheerful or gloomy? Is there a good rapport between students and faculty?

# ADDITIONAL RESOURCES

Have lunch with a student. Sit in on a class. Find out who decides on room-mates. How does the residential advisory system work? What are the meal plan choices? If you have time, arrange for a dorm stay; ideally, you'd want to be matched up with a sophomore or junior at the college. Try to talk to students who haven't been hired by the admissions office to sing the school's praises. Don't just ask whether they like the school, ask what they'd change if they could. And find out what they did last weekend. Remember: you're gathering data for that comparative anthropology book on campus cultures. Note your own reactions, too. Do you feel claustrophobic or cozy on an intimate New England campus? Fearful surrounded by hundreds of strangers in a university or excited by the vibrancy of a big city? Amber's M.'s experience at Amherst was neither unprecedented nor unusual; it simply confirms what I remind my clients: in the end, your gut feeling about a school is the most important observation of all.

When to go? Sure, you can visit colleges anytime, but those tanned bodies flipping frisbees might be summer-school imposters. Better to visit while college is in session, better still to visit when your own high school is on break. After all, you don't want to miss school and endanger your coursework: academic accomplishment is still the most criterion for admission to most schools.

One final suggestion: some families find it helpful to record impressions of each college visit on a comparison chart. You can download a sample form, along with additional questions you might want to ask, at www.25Months.com. Click on RESOURCES, then "College Visits." WHEN YOU GO:

**SOME PRE-DEPARTURE SUGGESTIONS TO MAKE YOUR TRIP EASIER;** the admissions department at most colleges can provide this information; contact them by e-mail.
- Find out when campus tours are scheduled and how long they last.
- If there are campus information sessions, when are they scheduled
- Can you arrange to sit in on a class? Have lunch with a student?

CONTINUED ON PAGE 84

# ADDITIONAL
# RESOURCES

## CAMPUS VISITS: CULTURAL ANTHROPOLOGY (CONTINUED)

**QUESTIONS FOR THE ADMISSIONS STAFF OR TOUR GUIDES:**
- How are students advised about what courses to take?
- Do students evaluate the professors?
- What percentage of students are housed on campus?
- Does financial aid impact admission decisions?
- How are wait-listed students handled?
- What personal qualities do students tend to have here?

**QUESTIONS FOR STUDENTS:**
- Why did you pick this college? Has it lived up to your expectations?
- What are the benefits and shortcomings of going here?
- If you could change one thing about the college, what would it be?
- What do you do for fun?
- What percentage of students are housed on campus?
- Does financial aid impact admission decisions?
- How are wait-listed students handled?
- What personal qualities do students tend to have here?

# NOTES:

Colleges visited:

West Coast:

_____

_____

_____

_____

Midwest:

_____

_____

_____

_____

East Coast:

_____

_____

_____

_____

# ADDITIONAL RESOURCES

## COLLEGE INTERVIEWS: SHOW YOUR PASSION

As you sit in the hallway, looking at your freshly shined shoes, awaiting your turn for "the most important interview ever," afraid this is a make-or-break moment that will determine your fate for the next four years, the previous candidate staggers out, eyes rolling. Then they call your name. Stomach churning, palms sweating, you greet an unsmiling interviewer. The first question you hear seems baffling.

Nervous? Sure. Terrified? Don't be.

Here's the truth: the college interview rarely makes or breaks an application.

It's not a test with right and wrong answers, it's a two-way street. The admissions officers aren't looking for reasons to exclude you from their campus-far from it. They see it as an opportunity to meet you in person and learn more about you. Take advantage of the situation!

Consider the interview as a chance to highlight your accomplishments, convey your passions, and explain the weakest part of your application.

Furthermore, it's okay to be a little nervous. Admit it. "I'm nervous because I'd really like to attend here." No interviewer expects a 17-year-old to have all the answers to life. It is okay to say you're undecided about a major; it shows you're ready to continue learning at college. Remember: if you know what you want to get across, no interviewer will be able to defeat you. If you're eager to talk about last year's research paper, it's your job to direct your answers to include that topic.

How much does the interview "count?" Think of it as an opportunity to explain irregularities in your transcript and to present yourself in a positive way. If the essay was your introduction, the interview is your "hello," giving a personal touch to dry academic statistics.

So, how best to prepare?

The two important traits to show are passion and initiative.

Go into the interview with a sense of what you want to emphasize about yourself and with a set of questions about the school not answered in the printed material. The interview is a dialogue, so plan to ask questions like "My high school's social life is dominated by the jocks but I'm looking for a more intellectual atmosphere. What is your college doing to foster intellectual discussion?" "What happens on a typical weekend?" "Do students talk about current issues?" "Tell me about the study abroad programs." "What is your [the interviewer's] connection to the college?" "Would you send your own child to this school?"

Some questions are predictable and you can prepare by writing out responses to sample questions, practicing with family, friends or in front of a mirror.

# ADDITIONAL RESOURCES

For example, you can expect to be asked why you want to attend this particular college. Have an answer ready that states your own academic and extra-curricular interests and your understanding that the school meets those interests.

Some other likely questions: What do you like to do in your free time? What have you enjoyed most about your high school years? What would you change about your school? How did you overcome difficulties in your most challenging class? Is your academic record an accurate gauge of your potential?

But there might be some "curveball" questions as well: What do you see when you get up in the morning and look in the mirror? What books have you found enjoyable but challenging? Whom do you admire? What makes you angry? How have you grown or changed? What three adjectives would your best friend use to describe you? Why? Which weaknesses would you like to improve? How do you respond to academic competition and pressure? What do you want from life?

Two final thoughts. It's a good idea to bring copies of your activities list and ask, as you conclude your interview, if you might leave one behind. That way, you'll feel less pressure to cover every activity in the 45 minute interview.

At the end of the session, ask for the interviewer's card so you can send a thank-you note when you get home. Try to include a reference to a point discussed in the interview.

## INTERVIEWING GUIDELINES
- Don't be shy, making the interviewer drag answers out of you.
- Keep responses honest…don't fake anything. If you don't know, it is best to say "Good question. I'd like to think about it and email a response tomorrow."
- Remain composed by taking a deep breath before answering.
- Ask what the interviewer means if you don't understand the question.
- Shake hands firmly with the interviewer and maintain eye contact. Smile. Project confidence by keeping your head up and shoulders back.
- Speak in complete sentences, avoiding colloquial expressions [anyways [should be anyway], like, whatever].
- Practice, practice with a friend, relative, teacher. This gives confidence and raises points you might have overlooked.
- Read the newspaper daily for 2-3 weeks before the interview in order to discuss issues of concern to you.
- Know what is on your application already, especially the contents of your essays.
- You do not have to reveal your first choice college, simply mention several you are applying to.

# ADDITIONAL RESOURCES

## PAYING THE BILL: ADVICE FROM A FINANCIAL PLANNER

**BY STEVE SHAPIRO, CPA, CFP,
CERTIFIED COLLEGE PLANNING SPECIALIST**

The college admissions process can be quite frustrating, puzzling and stressful. I'm confident that if you use some of the ideas in this chapter, you'll be able to reduce the impact of college costs. Start planning now...don't put it off.

Next to buying a house and funding your retirement, paying for college is the most expensive investment many parents will make. Fortunately, there are many ways to reduce the impact of college costs.

### ADVICE FOR STUDENTS

#### Choose Your Colleges Wisely

Choose a college that is a good match for you. Whether you do it on your own or with assistance from an educational consultant, choose a college that suites you – academically, socially, physically and emotionally. Failure to do so often results in a school change, which can be an expensive proposition.

Identify colleges that are a good fit for you that are not overwhelmed with applications or are a bit off the beaten path. This increases your chances of gaining admission and of receiving grants and scholarships.

#### Tips for Athletes

Be proactive. Don't wait to be contacted by college coaches. Unless you are a "blue-chip" high school athlete, college coaches outside of your immediate area don't know that you exist and therefore, can't recruit you. Instead, research the colleges that match your academic and athletic criteria and begin contacting the coaches yourself.

Be realistic about the level at which you can or should compete – division I, II, III, NAIA or Junior College. And start reaching out to college coaches in your sophomore or junior year. Don't wait until you are a senior.

# ADDITIONAL RESOURCES

**Apply for Scholarships**

Though private scholarships provide less than 3% of college expenses nationwide, many students win considerable amounts of money each year by following some variation of these tips:

1 Start with your high school counselor or scholarship coordinator for scholarship information
2 Search locally – service clubs such as Rotary, Soroptimist, Lions, Kiwanis, etc.
3 Consider religion, race, ethnicity, nationality, heritage, etc. in your scholarship searches.
4 Consider affinity groups, such as boy or girl scouts, 4H, etc.
5 You don't have to wait until you are a senior. Scholarships exist for students beginning in grade 6, so if you are a high school freshman, sophomore or junior, this is an ideal time to apply.
6 Use google to create your own scholarship search
7 Once admitted to a college, visit that school's web site to see if you might qualify for any of their scholarships.

**ADVICE FOR PARENTS**

**Apply for Financial Aid whether or not you think your family will qualify.**

1 Your student can qualify for the lower-interest student loans
2 Many expensive private colleges want to see your financial aid forms before they will award merit aid.
3 You can earn well over $100,000 and still qualify for need-based financial aid at many expensive private colleges or universities.

**Maximize Need-Based Financial Aid Potential**

Arrange family income and assets to qualify for the maximum amount of need-based aid possible. If your son or daughter doesn't qualify for need-based aid at a public college, they might qualify at an expensive private school.

This planning should ideally begin when your son or daughter is a sophomore in high school.

**Alternative Planning for High-Income/High-Net Worth Families**

For families, whose income and assets are too high to qualify for need-based aid, alternative planning can help reduce the impact of college costs. Options include in-

CONTINUED ON PAGE 90

# ADDITIONAL RESOURCES

creasing cash flow by increasing income or reducing expenses; reducing the amount of taxes being paid (money not spent on taxes can be used to help with college costs).

### Don't Be Afraid to Appeal the College's Offer

Once your student receives his or her acceptance letter and financial aid offer, it's perfectly okay to enter into a dialogue with the colleges in an effort to "sweeten" the offers.

To make this work, the student must offer the college a significant amount of "merit." In other words, they must really want your son or daughter on their campus.

Your student or family must have "special circumstances". These are legitimate financial conditions that exist in your family that affect your ability to pay for your student's education. Examples (the possibilities are endless):

• Mother or father lost their job or retired
• Unusually high medical expenses or family illnesses
• Younger sibling in expensive private high school
• An elderly relative is living with the family, creating a drain on the family's finances.
• Student has received a better offer from another school.

### SOME HELPFUL BOOKS AND WEB SITES

*Paying for College Without Going Broke* by Kalman Chany, Princeton Review. An excellent book on the entire process

*How to go to college ... almost for free* by Ben Kaplan, Waggle Dancer. An excellent book that guides you through the scholarship game

**www.finaid.org** is a good, all around web site for college planning

## THE AUTHOR

 **Judy McNeely** is the founder of *College Pathfinders*, with over 27 years of experience as an independent college counselor. She holds a BA in English from Stanford University, a Master of Library Science from UCLA, and has received additional training in college admissions. Currently living in Santa Cruz, California, she has nearly three decades of classroom experience in Washington and California schools, teaching high school French, Spanish and Library Media. Ms. McNeely was selected as a grader for the new SAT I essay. In addition, she is an active member of the National Association of College Admissions Counseling (NACAC), Pacific Northwest Association of College Admissions Counseling (PNACAC), Western Association of College Admissions Counseling (WACAC) and the Higher Education Consulting Association (HECA) .

Specific questions about this book, along with suggestions for future editions, should be addressed to the author via email at judybookdoc@collegepathfinders.com. I look forward to your feedback.